Do Parrots Have Pillows?

A Book About Where Animals Sleep

Written by Michael Dahl
Illustrated by Sandra D'Antonio

Content Consultant: Kathleen E. Hunt, Ph.D.
Research Scientist and Lecturer, Zoology Department
University of Washington, Seattle, Washington

Reading Consultant: Susan Kesselring, M.A., Literacy Educator
Rosemount-Apple Valley-Eagan (Minnesota) School District

PICTURE WINDOW BOOKS
MINNEAPOLIS, MINNESOTA

Animals All Around series editor: Peggy Henrikson
Page production: The Design Lab
The illustrations in this book were rendered in marker.

Picture Window Books
5115 Excelsior Boulevard
Suite 232
Minneapolis, MN 55416
1-877-845-8392
www.picturewindowbooks.com

Printed in the United States of America.

Library of Congress Cataloging-in-Publication Data
Dahl, Michael.
Do parrots have pillows? / written by Michael Dahl ; illustrated by
Sandra D'Antonio.
p. cm. — (Animals all around)
Summary: Introduces a number of different animals and where
they sleep.
ISBN 1-4048-0374-2 (pbk.) ISBN 1-4048-0104-9 (hardcover)
1. Animals—Habitations—Juvenile literature. [1. Animals—
Habitations.]
I. D'Antonio, Sandra, 1956— ill. II. Title.
QL756 .D33 2003
591.56'4—dc21
2002155020

Do Parrots Have Pillows?

No! Parrots have nest holes.

Parrots sleep in holes they find in trees. Parrots also climb inside the holes to lay their eggs. If a flock of parrots cannot find enough nest holes in a forest, some of the birds will not lay eggs.

4

Do bears have pillows?

No! Bears have dens.

Bears sleep all winter in snug, warm dens. A den can be a rocky cave, a hole dug in the ground, or a large, hollowed-out tree. Bears cubs are born in the den during the winter while their mother sleeps.

Do rabbits have pillows ?

No! Rabbits have warrens.

Rabbits live in a maze of underground tunnels called a warren. They sleep in special holes dug into the sides of the tunnels. Baby rabbits sleep in nests lined with soft leaves, moss, or clumps of their mother's fur.

8

Do eagles have pillows ?

No! Eagles have eyries.

Eagles build their eyries, or high nests, in tall trees or on the tops of cliffs. From their lofty perches, eagles can spy flashing fish or running rabbits down below. Eagles hunt during the day. At night, they rest in their eyries.

"Do beavers have pillows?"

No! Beavers have lodges.

Beavers build lodges of dried mud and branches in a river, pond, or lake. A beaver can slip inside the lodge by swimming through a hidden, underwater opening. A room in the top of the lodge stays warm and dry for sleeping.

Do bees have pillows ?

No! Bees have hives.

A hive is a home where bees store honey, pollen from flowers, and bee eggs. Bees are very busy during the day. At night, they rest quietly in the hive.

Do snails have pillows ?

No! Snails have shells.

Snails sleep deep in their hard, curving shells during hot, bright days. At night or during damp, cool mornings, snails slowly slip through green gardens, carrying their homes on their backs.

Do spiders have pillows?

No! Spiders have webs.

A spider spins its web with thin threads called filaments. The filaments come from the spider's body. Even when the spider rests, its knees and legs can feel when a tiny, buzzing fly disturbs the web.

Do bats have pillows ?

No! Bats have caves.

Bats sleep upside down, with their sharp toes gripping the rocky roof of a cave. Hundreds of bats sleep together. They keep each other warm with their soft, furry bodies.

Do people have pillows ?

Yes!
People have
pillows
and blankets
and beds,
and sheets to
pull over
their warm,
sleepy heads.

Where Animals Sleep

Some animals sleep up high.

the roof of a cave   bat

the hole of a tree   parrot

a rocky cliff   eagle

Some animals sleep down low.

a cozy, warm den   bear

a soft, safe tunnel   rabbit

Some animals make their own places to sleep.

a honeycombed hive   bees

a web of sticky strings   spider

a log home in the water   beaver

Some animals never leave their homes.

a hard, shiny shell   snail

Words to Know

den—a place for some animals to sleep, such as a cave, underground hole, or hollow tree. Bears, wolves, and coyotes have dens.

eyrie—a bird's nest built high in a tree or on the side of a cliff or rocky mountain

filament—a long, thin string

flock—a group of birds

hibernate—to deeply sleep or rest quietly during the winter

lodge—a beaver's home of mud, logs, and sticks, built in the water

warren—a network of underground tunnels built by rabbits for safety and sleeping

Index

To Learn More

At the Library

Meade, Holly. *A Place to Sleep.*
New York: Marshall Cavendish, 2001.

Showers, Paul. *Sleep Is for Everyone.*
New York: HarperCollins, 1997.

Swanson, Diane. *Animals Can Be So Sleepy.*
New York: Greystone Books, 2001.

Zolotow, Charlotte. *Sleepy Book.*
New York: HarperCollins, 2001.

On the Web

FactHound offers a safe, fun way to find Web sites related to this book. All of the sites on FactHound have been researched by our staff.
www.facthound.com

1. Visit the FactHound home page.

2. Enter a search word related to this book, or type in this special code: 1404801049.

3. Click the FETCH IT button.

Your trusty FactHound will fetch the best Web sites for you!